A Place Inside

A Place Inside

poems
Judith Adams

GRAYSON BOOKS
West Hartford, Connecticut
graysonbooks.com

Dedication

Ann Scriven
who throughout my childhood
recited poetry to her dog in the room above mine
Repetitive thump of a tail and muffled voice

Acknowledgments

Some of the poems in this book are from previous books by Robin Press. Those poems are "Springing the Hill," "I Wanna Die Nice and Easy," "Love Letters Only" and "Opening Doors." "Walking the Dogs" was published in *The Poetry of Dogs* by J. A. Allen in London.

I would like to thank Grayson Books for publishing *A Place Inside* and Ginny Connors for her patience and sensibility. Additional thanks go to the community on Whidbey Island for their enduring support and the Pacific Northwest for its fresh mountain air and vibrant love of poetry.

Contents

Uncertainty

Even before I knew what
uncertainty really meant
I conjured catastrophe
at the school gate
eager for the green Morris Minor
that might never come.
An eviction notice taped to the front door.
The global inbreath for the terminal
Checkmate; the queen has had enough.
Our parents lived through a war.
They were part of the Greatest Generation.
They had us to name them but what will
we be called, and by whom?

Roots

They spread from God's apple cellar—
words of heavy cargo and myth.
Created my bones. Our bones.

From our shared womb,
I'm left searching for my sea-faring brother.
We were a sibling assortment of weeds.

On frosty days the gate swung open
to greening fields, to moors, stone walls,
mist threading hedgerows,

the kick of a cow, gallop of a horse
and the lark's praise for the sun.
All things I loved, as I love the human face.

Writing Postcards to Voters in Texas

Ahmed lives in San Antonio.
Maria Jose Chavez, Austin.
Jadon Alvarez and Stacy Maldonado,
Groves, Texas.
I cross them off, but not without lifting my pen—
would a prayer be more appropriate?
They must tell their friends
(the script says six).
Supposing they don't have any,
supposing they are alone
and I am causing them pain?
Their names are rich in imagery.
I don't want them to think
they are random or that all I care
is to push the agenda.
I am using a fountain pen
that might make them think
I care enough to spare the ink,
I care enough to let the address dry
before turning the card over.
I know by heart the telephone number
to call, mid-September, for early voting locations.
I want to connect.
Maybe if I beat a drum
or put on music they might like
or shut my eyes to see them
in their kitchens reading this card
while turning mushrooms in the pan
thinking to themselves *I wonder*
who wrote this card, how sweet!
Or tossing it into the garbage with a grunt.
We are named at our birth.
One small piece of music
for the universe.

A Mother's Continuum

I did not pause beyond the joy
of how you would laugh,
run wild and free.
I was creator, artist.
The symphony of it, the brilliance!
Your future yet no impact!
Salad days of summer knees,
picnics, expeditions and in school
slowly climbing the grades.
And still I am such—
seventy-two and holding
my original bundle in a worried compartment,
your helicopter hurtling haphazardly
toward the hurricane in Texas,
kitted out in rescue gear
and descending wire.
I imagine you chatting above the din,
your new wife and children back at home.
Tipping forward and back,
landing noisily at the base,
ducking the blades,
as I am gardening, and unsettled.

Hummingbird

If anything has been given to us
so we would believe in heaven,
it is the sound of the staccato in the air
of the hummingbird's little ruby body
halted at an invisible crossroad,
its fanning wings held between a
heartbeat and a ninety degree turn towards the east.

This summer I found one in the house,
its needle beak pounding at the window
above the stairs. Who would believe
I had it in my hands?
I was so close to its divinity.
I inspected it as I would
a tiny rose window in a tiny church.

Its heart must be the size of a linseed.
Its little head no bigger than a blueberry,
and its red costume, slightly iridescent,
is like a poppy under rolling clouds
before a storm. I ran to the garden door
to watch it gain height from my fingers,
the way joy does
when it has nothing to do with possessions.

Lost Mittens

Children leave themselves
in bright colors dotted
around the universe.

Like crocuses or wildflowers,
lost mittens blossom
on the fence line

above snowdrifts in the park.
You can imagine the cold
little hand heading home,

the difficult conversation,
retracing steps across the morning.
Still none the wiser

straying into a sad territory of loss.
On the last shift the old man
placed each one on the pickets,

he must have thought how tiny
they are. Must have thought
how the years fool one, how we think

there is plenty of time to change.
There under the moon, mittens,
like a long prayer flag,

messages of hope in the cold.

The End of Summer 2020

Ask history for forgiveness.
If you don't know what you are here for,
sleep on the edge of the sea,
let it breathe for you.
Let the wind enter the garden with a ballot
As apples and pears drop, hold onto their ripeness.
Their willingness to let go
is all the politics you need.

Anonymous

On the BBC late one night
Anne Duffy, the English Poet Laureate,
said Anon is a woman
who locked her poems in a drawer.
If the poet did put a name to anything,
it had to be male, like George Sand.
Anonymous has endured since the cruel
burning of her sisters—
their poems were healing
and a threat to the ledgers of power.
Still, she flees the most
despicable weapon of war.
For her the angels weep.
As for the perpetrators,
even the devil is ashamed.

What Holds Me Together

Is not childhood's muddled accounts,
diffuse and fleeting like the train going north
from robin's egg to heather.
Nor jack in the pulpit's shocking
thrust through the forest's growth,
or wind on the craggy moor blustering my name.

Opening the gate on frost keeps me in love with a god
who might like me and my difficult angel.
The swath of mountains stretches the eye
to upper realms of blessing
and the first woolly sweater in the chill of fall.
A light in a window of books;
passing by, I might like to meet the readers.
The pure silk of a kiss,
the uncensored laughter of children,
a human face that takes the soul off guard,
blows it open, in that glimpse the discarnate,
truer than comforts that can't quite hold me together.

Ode to the Candle

In your body, summer flowers
heaped bee by bee,
golden, smooth and waxy.
Your perfect shape intact.
The alpha flame outside your body
molds you from the inside.
Your walls become sculpture,
a work in progress.
You glow deeper from your depths.
Your body withers as the aged room
grows wider and more radiant.
Nothing now but pure light of omega.

Pomme de Terre

This is the day to
find potatoes.
The wind has set
everything off.
Underneath feathers
peck sideways;
a lovely madness
in the garden.
I am digging for apples
of the earth, pale moons
asleep in darkness.

This is what the
angels do on a
windy night.
They dig us up
and smile. For we
have grown at
different rates
into all shapes
and sizes.

Homeless Woman in Asheville, NC

That night there was drumming in town
all and sundry beating skins.
Old and young dancing the blues,
dancing the rhythm of their bones.
Tucked in the crowd a homeless woman.
The white jurisdiction of her
eyes roaming in the landscape of her face,
her body slumped in an old stroller and
under threadbare blankets,
sequined shoes from a bride's discarded moment.
I asked her if I could take a photo.
She pushed them further out into the cold
for my benefit, and for her own satisfaction,
her own thrilled inspection.
Without toothpaste or moisturizer or
any elaborate foreplay, she settled
to the sound of everyone else's living,
heading upwards in her dream
her feet dangling celestial sparkles.

Love Letters Only

The Almighty is frugal.
She does not accept checks,
only half interested in IOUs,
ignores twitter and
regrets bore her.
She would rather
you had a wild night
on the town.
When you arrive at the
famous gates,
don't fumble in your
pockets for
love letters
you never sent.

I Will Have Her Back

the person I used to be
in the descent of my thirties,
raw for the God I found there.
The startling news of philosophies,
speaking for the first time.
Head over heels for inquiry,
the cocky denouncement of the old family.
Now Sunday afternoon in my sixties,
I think of her wild appetite for truth.
The affair is not over. I will have her back
with her loud-mouthed yearning,
her calf love of the divine.

How We Manage

There is no steady place to stand.
We call in our animals;
the hovering hummingbirds,
the owl that knows us,
and the eagle from a nesting height.
Mountains bloom on the sea
in participating prayer.
When bad news arrives, we spin
in jeopardy of losing the most
treasured in our midst.
The sick ones rally
and live the way we all meant to.
Ambitions slip into dawn's
overwhelming beauty.
We are all undocumented;
no one has the right papers.
When the door slams
and you are heading to a
compulsory appointment,
how do you find love poems
among old tins and peels?
Here is one: a pale checkout girl
works through the night,
arrives home as her baby wakes at dawn.
She covers him in kisses.
This is how we manage.

Second Wind

You will recognize it
by the shoes you refuse to wear,
company you cannot keep.

When the second wind
batters the north windows,
let it in. Admit its full force.

Now is not the time to shrink.
Your posture operatic, your mood excited,
you can bloom and bloom again.

Belly Flop

You do an outrageous
belly flop.
So what if
not every dive
into the river
is graceful.

Arms and legs
akimbo, you go
for whatever
the mud and
the slow
running water
and slippery
reeds would
give you.

Don't mind
my laughter.
It is pure
joy for the
sacrament of risk,
the river faring
unprepared,
the leap into
a stinging descent.

I would never accuse
God of holiness.
He knows
what it takes
to enter
the heart.

Sex Shop

On holiday with friends
we went to one of notable reputation.

Launched into its extensive stock.
The serving girl, big-busted, red cheeked and elated,

picked out selections like a chocolatier
exclaiming nuance—

a neon pink replica 'true friend'
for excitement and durability.

Of course, we had our budget to consider.
But for companionship like this, why scrimp?

Go for top of the line. After all, batteries can run out
in mid-delight. The girl was intent, weighing integrity

and drawn into our uncensored amusement.
We finally selected brands

our mothers would have winced over
and proclaimed perverted.

Flamenco

A warrior learns to dance,
to balance passion
and strength,

to suspend emotions
in elegant architecture
of wings before descent.

Clapping begins
and ignites contradictions
wrestling in the heart.

A single rhythm gathers momentum
in the body, in the voice,
that destroys the whiner,

the grumbler, and calls
to those who do not fear
what the world insists upon.

We all have it in us;
the proud protester, too muscular
for mundane inclination.

Evocative resilience,
defiant in the tides of love.
Explosion of counterpoint

articulated pounding feet,
unabridged expression,
surrendering to the dance

that ends when it ends.

The Barn

I must have been eight,
strong enough to open the barn door
next to the milking herd,
noses down into fields of hay.
It was the beginning of Autumn.
The floor was swept, dust collecting
in places outside of the broom.
I could smell the spade, the rake,
the pitch fork, and overalls
hanging by one strap.
Straw was piled to the rafters,
and swallows were noisily preparing
for their wind journey south.
Scanning the dark shadows,
I look up to a small window,
partly covered by cobwebs.
Unblinking, a white barn owl
stared into me, into who I was
at eight. Before such scrutiny
I froze, unable to turn away.

The Great Escape

Out of his baby bed
in his fox onesies
he heads down the stairs.

Each step a defiant proclamation.
Naughty, naughty, naughty,
he scolds himself

well-satisfied at his delivery,
foreshadowing the day
he will get wheels, get away

from oversight. Adventure
begins with mutinous advance,
fortitude for freedom,

skepticism of authority
and the humming motor
of risk, risk, risk.

Walk with a Three-Year-Old

He runs into the woods,
jeans enveloping a tiny bum
of forward determination,
shoulders raised for balance.
His Shetland sweater fern height,
into moss, root and heave,
like a shepherd takes on the slope,
hell-bent on finding his sheep.
As we come out into the open
a diminutive oracle proclaims
We made it!
like a content old man
turning to his wife after a lifetime.

Children at Home During the Coronavirus

In the kitchen the status quo in tatters.
Uncertainty scrambles to recalibrate
from rhythms that held the family aloft.
Schools are closed, parks padlocked.
A dish put down to fix a shoelace,
and dreams told at the breakfast table
are sanctified, for there is no rush for the door,
no clatter down the stairs to the bus.
The intonation we choose
is how the day unfolds.
This long period of uncertainty
is also a time of possibility.
Our levity now is the children's future dance.
It is hard to die to anything when we have so
often forgotten how to be alive,
how to captain our days from within.

Complicated

You are the complicated one
who argues the toss
and refuses to go to bed.
You are the one
who ruins the atmosphere in class
and can't see the point of
limiting one to a symbol.
Why not a vast sea
between mountains or great forest
grown from one seed?
Out of boredom you fall off your chair.
Specialists hand out reports
naming everything that you do
with initials. You are the complicated one
who spills the sauce because dragons
are under your feet.
The whole household is awakened
by the darkness of your nightmares.
You are the tiresome one
who grows up with a battle cry.
The complicated one
who will not barter imagination
for comfort or half-loving.
You are the one
who marries three times,
mistaking each one for God.
Do not take your shoes off
at the temple door. Your journey
is longer, more difficult,
more beautiful than that.

First Born

The primordial starlit language.
Your desire for another existence.
I might have adapted, I might have
found a story that would fit your origin.
Holding you in that first bundled,
stunned mystery of love
your almond eyes roamed the prospect
of my face in doubt,
as if the proverbial stork
skipped a house, even a country.
The placenta cut, its watery
conversation past recall.
We gave you everything we thought was good—
a pony, life in the country,
a gentler school that cradled sensitivity.
In the end the widening gulf
got the better of us, flared up in ideology,
abandoned family and drifted from
the warmth we'd thought enduring.
Liturgy of womb is the fount of mystery.
A prenatal syntax that in the end banished our love.
You and your children walk away.
The immutable umbilical tether
coiled and silenced in my heart.

Two Reasons for Weeping

In the isolation of Covid-19
there was no standing
by the hand-dug graveside.
We took to cars, an old fire engine,
bold literary placards of farewell,
apple blossoms and Tibetan flags
secured handle to the handle.
Love can never be silenced,
birdsong at dawn is proof of that.
How can we express deep affection
from car windows, pray or sing
with the engine going?
We crawled in a circular drive-by,
a chain of hearts leaning toward
the assembled family; grandchildren
with small bouquets of gathered forget-me-nots,
and her beloved's blue sweater.
Her body wrapped in a white shroud
of local prayers and flowers,
cradled in a wooden hammock,
motionless like an illuminated pagan saint
of diminutive supremacy.
Sun flooding her death cottage,
April wind circling the gravestones.
More beauty than I could have imagined—
and she knew it.
As I drove home, pink blossoms
levitating from the car's roof and bonnet,
my daughter called.
Mom, I am having a girl.
I wept for two reasons.

In the Aftermath

The train leaned and switched tracks in approach.
Row upon row of soot-black windowless houses.
Hushed history lodged in a child's shapeless understanding—
war happened out a compartment window.
Steam bloomed, doors slammed,
and porters shouted *London, Liverpool Street.*

In forbidden moments I climbed to the attic,
holding up the lid for private viewing.
Mothballs like white snowberries
over the breast, buttons and wings
of my father's Royal Air Force gabardine,
the household determined to forget.
Wind rattled black-out blinds.
We crouched on the staircase in pajamas
to spy on the adults' raucous recovery
from sugar ration, years of scarcity and worry.
Eclairs stuffed with condensed milk,
whipped margarine and camp coffee,
sweet elixir we harvested at dawn
from the wreckage of the dining room.
In my five-year-old heart, I believed we were safe.
I had post office saving stamps.
Two and sixpence to keep us fed
if war broke out again.

English Teacher

Growing up in the fifties was to grow up
at the knees of adult sarcasm and
their determination to stamp out
the catastrophe of our fledgling self-love.
The survivors hung out at the back of the class.
You came in with blue eye shadow,
fuchsia lipstick, and believed
in our half-cocked ideas. You helped them bloom.
And when asked to approached the blackboard,
we were all winners. In order to move freely,
in order to improvise, to recite
what was in our boots, in our hearts,
you had us push back the desks.
Delicious liberation.
In that free space we learned
language has wings to fly.

The Birth of Brigid

Biden had just been elected.
Democracy wavered in uncertainty.
The pandemic clung to our doorstep.
And we were anxious.
Mother was to deliver in mask, shield,
and with the feminine force of the moon.
The infant hurled herself
down the birth canal like a rogue wave.
Already she had her own signature.
Checking the contours of the armored face
of her mother for familiar resonance,
Brigid searched for the soft breast,
the closest planet she knew.

Evening Reckoning

We slide the boats into the reeds
skirting the shore.
Laying our paddles flat
for conversation;
the problem of ego
the struggle to manage it
is like holding a
balloon under water.
You have to learn indulge it.
as if it were a child at play.

On the home stretch
smug with my own agility,
I bump the dock
toss my left leg over,
for a thorough dousing.
The boat fills with water
obstinate with tonnage
and the plain fact,
the existential bruise,
that I am an old lady.

Kayaking

Hauling the boat over rocks
your unshod feet tenderized by barnacles
and embalmed seaweed's oily flowers
cushioned in a rusty under green.
Take all of yourself, your whole history,
the past hour's neurosis into this small
container and be no more than blue,
to where the water is turning silver
at the meeting of currents.
When you are far enough away
from the cabin, the dock, the washing
drying in the afternoon,
let the paddles rest and rock
and be taken.
You are more than you ever imagined.
Look at the horizon in the mist below
the mountains, the silent islands
communicating from familiar distance.
Can you go on living your life
on the shore as if the kitchen of things mattered?
Untangle from the morning's imperative,
paddle out of your mind
to an intimacy beyond yourself.

Resting the Paddles

On the water's shifting surface
a mother and baby seal
their oily heads glistening
above the glimmering salt in
disappearing counterpoint
with a hidden world that
holds them in playful intimacy.
Two whiskered noses up again,
bouncing in sea-soaked calligraphy.
Oblivious of self-awareness that
so complicates our lives.
I refuse to rest in routine,
to drift in my steeply hurrying days.

All the small movements I have missed.

Walking the Dogs

It is no common
ritual to be out again
on the headlands and hoarfrost.
To follow pathways into mist
and circle a cursive language
across the cold hills.

To sniff the still warm nuggets
of night where the relaxed
body of the fox
has woven red
down the long slope
towards the woods.

They bounce back toward me
checking that I am happy and
coming along the ridge too.
The sheep dog douses himself
in deer droppings, seductive as
Chanel No. 5.

Turning toward home
and away from the wind
I call out to them.
Finally, they rise out of the
echo of their own names.
Ears flapping towards me.

The Great Ascent

It was unforgettable the scene.
A tense caravan of elephants
escaping Burma in WW II,
loaded with refugees navigating
an impossible wall of jungle.
Titanic feet squeezing from one
foliage groove to the next,
steeply sloping to the summit.
Tense for the sight of the most
bold, most beloved elephant
to appear over the ridge.
He did not know
if he had made the right decision.
There was the risk of sliding
back to their deaths.
Over the ridge the first gray continent of a head,
forward trunk taking the brunt of weight and balance.
One by one, safe on the open ledge
to the sight of refuge in the valley below.

Taking Jesus Down from the Cross

It took the locals
getting together,
much discussion,
and heartache.
The body limp
and darkness fallen
below the fulcrum.
Hands working
to unravel rope that held
his pinioned body.
Their stomachs lurching
with disbelief, rage,
guilt and despair.
His love
for the townspeople,
charged in the
Roman air.

Sabbatical

for Steph

The word sabbatical comes from the Sabbath—
holy occupation, easy to squander.
For years you have juggled joint schedules,
childcare, dog care, and Ultimate Frisbee.
A yoyo triangle: Portland bus,
Vancouver car, your women's group
wedged between non-profit exhaustion
and the midnight arrival of your lover
as you toss for early rise and shine.

Now is the time to write your book.
Now is the time to resist your dawn dash
to the kitchen, calculating how much protein
the family is not consuming.
Nights of policing homework,
commiserating over the vicissitudes
of teenage dating.

It's time to clear a path inward,
fill it with wildflowers. Take off your shoes,
walk on the beach in the morning.
Wander the countryside,
open gates into quiet fields
Explore the slow region of divinity,
the unstructured conversation with the One
who holds the patent of the universe.

For Mary Oliver

Mary Oliver lived her words.
I would rather eat chicken bones
and write than have a profitable life of things.

I loved her because she, too, worried, a lot.
I loved the way she brought a swan into vivid view

Few can write one line
that catches the population's breath.

I am forlorn.
She no longer walks her beloved dunes.
nor lies beneath the wind.

Her words are scattered in the bark of trees,
and in August blackberries.

How will God resist her—the dead clamoring
to get a glimpse of her arrival.

A Man with a Poem

Searching the digital warehouse
for philosophical clips,
I found a young man from Scotland
in his untidy house,
reciting Stafford's poem
"A Story that Could Be True."

A selfie bard,
inches from his own face.
Somebody's boy in a
bookish sweater,
in love with the message,
not with fashionable intonation.

The poem bursts inside him,
outside the wind's
dying down
over the moors,
the village post office
closing its doors.

The poem is in weekend attire,
relaxed, measured, passionate.
And from the cosmos,
William Stafford,
breaking down
in tears.

The Poem You Are Not Writing

tugs at a reluctant morning.
Barelegged and half-undressed,
it drags you to its lair.
Words crop up like nettles,
the blackbird's song or
the wind's volume of silver
metaphors perch in the poplar tree.
The poem you are not writing
is thrashing around, causing trouble,
roaming back alleys,
and when it finds you,
shoves you up against the wall
until you empty your pockets
and give it everything.

Abundance

Abundance leaps from the Latin
abundia; the verb abundare;

a shit load, three bags full!
A host, quantities, scores, a slew,

oodles. Single mellow
moon and sovereign sun.

Night sounds from the
marshes that catch your shoe.

Lace and light of matins
diffuse in a chapel of bird song.

The countryside looks
through your window,

              your open door—

Do you have any idea
how expensive you are,

the industry it takes to keep
you amazed, and grateful?

Oh, Lordy Lord!

A Place Inside

You have a place inside of you
no one can touch.
It's where your tools are kept.
In this divine workshop
you chisel at a raw day
in deep devotion to yourself,
and there you allow some unruliness,
your share of sore complaint.
And there you follow
your own footsteps
through the dark.

Birthday Poem

Doesn't it seem odd, to survive we need a job,
a set of complex circumstances?
Birds are happy feeding their young
with what the earth gives them.
The sea comes to the shore
with her kingdom of unseen beauty,
and the river, what a metaphor she is.
We are digital. We ain't half clever
with our arsenal of Google,
burgeoning robots that will
surely sweep us closer to new mystery.

There are things people believe are real.
God, for instance, but no one has proof.
We know how a seed grows, the light, etc.
But even a microscope can't explain why.
Our lives are mind-blowing and fleeting.
What great-grandchild will remember
the canvas of our thoughts?

Today is my birthday.
I want to be propelled into a realm
that is a true experience of love.
The dying will tell you about that.
Every day I need this exact day.
Yesterday I was immature,
today I get another step.

Breakfast from the Armchair

In your full-bodied life,
you never ate oatmeal.
Now its glutinous softness

cools as your limbs
withdraw into fragile bones.
The wood fire lit,

you count the pills
with a rug over your knees,
your walking stick leaning by the chair.

Companioned by winter
and your illness with its new demands.
We dip our spoons through the cream

as if we were on a train
headed for a destination
we did not choose.

The kettle whistles.
I have no way to save you
as you journey from here to there.

Your little dog curved into you
on the daybed, you consider
how the garden moves,

how the bamboo loves its life,
how one day it will shift in the
wind without you.

Last Day's Work

Emaciated, reduced in baggy trousers,
each upward step unbalanced by fragility.
Your walking stick
taking the weight of your illness.
Colleagues lean forward to receive you,
to guide your slow travel
towards the conference room.
Lawyers assemble in silence
sensing their own demise.
You arrange your brittle bones
in the armchair, propped with pillows.
Your mind, powered by your spirit
and formidable intellect,
negotiates longer than your body can tolerate.
You fight for the sake of a
small organization, from the muscular
victory of an industrial bully.
I am your wife, watching my
superstar serve for the last time,
his giant heart surfacing
to meet the terror of the
dreaded inevitable.

Prolong the Winter

Do not rush the buds to open in the orchard.
Prevent the birds from filling the garden with song,
Keep the wheelbarrow locked in ice
among white tears of snow drops.
I want to walk on the frozen pond
with my heart groaning and creaking,
I want to stay under the blankets with the
sound of the wind from the north
in the wilderness of your leaving.
Spring has promise but the
promise I want to make is to the
rawness of life, that
like a river floods through and
makes the reeds lie flat,
the mud shift into deep valleys,
in its wake the heart broken open.
Let the cold and the tender light
work on every tissue until
with each miraculous breath
I walk again across greening fields.

And We'll Adorn His Body

Do not take him away
with shining shoes of strangers
to a somber black display.
Leave him, and we'll adorn his body.
Let the musicians come.
Sit among flowers, candles
and the voice that remains in the room.
Let the ones he found so hard to leave
linger in calm as January mist hovers
in the garden, The heron flies
close to the chimney.
Under the moon, birds hush
in dripping calligraphy of branches.
Wrap him in a saffron shroud
and include in the pocket a poem.
Lay him in noble majesty.
The widow sings a requiem,
the door opens and closes,
villagers arrive with stories and
laughter and feasting.
Friends with shovels approach the grave,
the young doing most of the work, the old
digging in half-rhythm for their own transition.
And in the downpour, amazing grace
to bring him from his worldly house
to the place we speculate to be this or that.
In the slow largo of descent upon boughs of cedar,
white flowers are thrown into his arms
and across his body.

Your Old Sweater

Your sweater, cabled and woolly
took a whole sheep, I suspect for your six-foot four heart.
Late in the evening as chill settles in the garden
I sometimes lend my men friends your sweater
To see it moving again, lifting a glass of wine,
toasting friends, it swamps them.
Fit only for a large sheltering man.
I like to pick it up in the closet by mistake
as I look for something to wear without you.
I breathe into its knitted furrows for the scent of safety.
From inside the heavy stitches
I can hear your sonorous voice
as if we were skin on skin
on a rainy Sunday afternoon.

When a True Father Dies
for Ken

There is a deep rumbling of loss,
final closing of a dependable door
and a sheltering embrace.
A true father is solid like the oak in the middle of a field
in full extent of itself, where sheep huddle
beneath branches of refuge.
A man does not rise out of muscle,
but from what is in his heart.
In the morning he gets up, reveling in possibility,
robust for the day to lay demands on the table
for the union. A true father brings back the world
shaped and organized, and does not leave you
without tools and a workshop, the light still on.

Visit to the Doctor

She has my weight, blood pressure,
and list of failed medications.
What is my pain level out of ten?
Her fast fingers wait to classify my
existence on a screen.
Her young face is oblivious
to the bend I have just rounded,
the diminishing road ahead.
What number knocks me out?

Ask me instead who I am,
what my mornings are like,
if I am working towards a future,
who in my life has just died?
If you don't have time, and you are
backing out of the room with your computer,
at least ask me if I drink alone.

Next time let's begin with the Bushman greeting.
Good Day, I saw you coming from afar
and I am dying of hunger.

Letter to My CPA

Dear Joanne,
I hired you on the fancy 17th floor—you were going to hold my hand.

I don't seem to have pages 8, 9, 11, 18 or 19 of your thirty
sheets of questions with no index. It does not look good.

Do I have "dependents?" Yes, of course.
we all do; everywhere we turn.
If you mean children under twenty-six, say so.

Papers shuffle into themselves
evading eye contact, elusive and vindictive.

Medical costs, how many, how much.
Panic. No receipts, only scraps of purgatory,
if you think in pictures. Tell me they are white swans,
and I'll gladly count them.

I have torn the perforated lines on the1099.
And what good is the biggest fucking calculator
to satisfy decimal points, tiny crumbs of a dollar?
So next year, Joanne,
I'm going to hire a gardener,
someone from the ground floor.

We can talk about flowers,
where seeds can best be planted,
how new grass needs the sun.
We'll discuss the wind in the pampas grass
and how the fig tree loves the secluded stone
on which it leans, and then we can talk about robins
and other local birds. By that time, tax season
will have vanished among blossoms and nettles.

Goodbye

Today you packed up the car and left.
Tonight, as I drove into the garage
the light you fixed went on,
so you will always be in the garage,
in the exhaust of my hot red car,
and magnificently in my bedroom.
I don't know how long it will take,
how many nights opening the windows
before my body calms down
from the gift of your touch.
Now all I can think to do
is to patrol the streets at night
in a slinky dress.
Instead, I am meditating.
It will never be as liberating
as the moment we flew up the stairs.

First Flight with My Son

The multi-dialed cockpit
is to hold us beyond terra firma.
Beyond the foothills and desert.

In its reluctant throat the propeller
collects sound and we move backward,
swing around, and bounce across the tarmac

toward the windsock's pulsing lamentation.
In a holding zone your deep voice
contacts the stiff tower

and we are leaning toward the clouds,
lifting and floating over sagebrush,
curds of snow mapping below.

Surprising the way we go on mounting the miraculous
sky together, peering beneath the wing,
like they do in movies, marking the railway to the west.

You, who journeyed my interior waters,
are now free to follow the dry riverbank.
You are reaching for life at the controls.

Suspended in currents of air
we are held in the presence
of our perfect and imperfect love.

You throttle back and
level out,
in the buffeting winds.

Left Quadriplegic in a Farm Accident, 2000 Died 2020

for David

I am looking for a place in the house
to write this poem.
I want to find a sunny spot where I can see
the trees and grasses moving in a lilt of wind.
I want to find a chair big enough to hold sorrow.
You never meant to leave the sight of birds
turning silver in the sun. You wanted to take
the cows that turned towards you as you entered the barn,
and the moon gliding through fields
in the milking hour's fragrance that clung to your clothes.
There is no part of the house that describes
your courage, no window that captures your journey.
I am sitting in the kitchen.
The workplace of the house seems appropriate.
Here I can see you in your boots holding a wrench
as you proclaim some extraordinary wisdom
that takes us off-guard and demands
our speechless response.
I need to go to the headlands to walk as far as an open field
occupied by owls, hawks and fireflies lifting the air.
This is where I fall to my knees.
This is the spot of sacred prayer
for those who turn the soil for life
and in the dark corridors of tragedy
stay faithful to beauty.

My Mother and the Bishop

Your 1950's dress clinched at the waist,
your eyes lifted to the fresco
standing in the sturdy pew
that separated us from God
in the church's damp restraint.
Our bare knees scratched
stiff stitches on the prayer stool.
Devotion
in the alteration of your voice.
But It all changed one morning
after you wrote to the Bishop,
asking him what he did all day.
From what you could see,
he was not tending his flock.
The official answer arrived on
embossed paper, a pedantic
exegesis of the urgency
of office work and jurisdiction.
God toppled from your heart.
Except for carols at Christmas.

Mother

She stood in the doorway,
a frail welcome wagon,
a single autumn leaf.
The kettle on, biscuits,
like repeated stories,
in the same battered tin.
How long was I staying,
Would I always live in America?
She flipped through the newspaper
and fixed on an ad
as if it were the editorial.
Sipped her whisky,
then announced it was high time
for a drink. The moon hung
in the courtyard. She shut the doors,
jabbing with the wrong key,
perplexed and irritated,
clinging to the banisters
as if a strong wind was delaying
her voyage in the last,
fierce currents of her life.
We have mostly locked horns,
my own self in her struggles,
her categoric conclusions,
her emphatic declarations.
In my panic to find the exit,
a high-speed train home,
I am plagued by sadness
and by my own heartlessness.
She appeared at the top of the stairs,
without her teeth, her face
collapsed and tiny;
gnarled bark of a tree
peering down at me,
an old mountain woman.
I loved her more than anything

Down to Zero

my mother at ninety-six

Last night she told my sister
I am in the best part of my life
because I am down to zero.

It was an odd kind of wisdom.
She trawls through her unhitched psyche,
childhood injustices, old loves,
pedaling her attachments
like wisps of thoughts in the wind.
Some people say what a waste
when the mind goes AWOL.
Life in not worth living in senility.
Once, I would have agreed
but now I see she travels
through the challenging bardo
people speak of, into every corner and nook
of her existence, like someone with
a duster happily cleaning her soul,
repeatedly thanking all and sundry.
We knew where to find her
on a Friday at the hairdresser's
under hooded heat.
How tired she sometimes looked.
We watched her smother her face in moisturizer.
Now she likes to eat it.
She is my great teacher again.
sweetly accepting her peripheral world.
When the noble hour arrives, she will slip
imperceptibly into wide open territory.
And knowing her as I do, she'll be
annoyingly smug about the times she did believe.

Last Visit

I walk under winged purpose magpies,
one for sorrow two for joy.
Hedge rows pocketing fields of frost

slope into the valley's welcome, mud puddles
and eggs for sale. I want to give her
the day's fresh air to soar the summits of her life.

She is clinging to a prolonged winter
decomposing the old growth of her strength
on a bed that crackles with compression and release.

Oddly random on the white wall,
photos of family, dogs and ribbons.
The only active possession a bib to catch puréed peas.

Someone else has chosen the radio station.
I want to bring her the sound of the wind,
Instead I take her bony cheeks into my hands;

shock surfacing in her blue eyes
a never spoken inquiry.
How can I respond to a hidden question

that belongs to angels?
Like a sea otter into saltwater,
she disappears into shallows of sleep.

Scattering Mom's Ashes Under the Quince

You have been on the kitchen counter
in the midst of household activity,
unpaid bills and preparations.
A perfect place, we all agreed.
I forgot about you there so your opinion
did not follow me into the pantry,
nor did I burn anything.
Yesterday afternoon I went
outside to the quince that you
bought because you said every
garden should have one and
now the quinces keep me busy for a week,
which you would have enjoyed.
I scattered you there.
I did not want you on the surface
though on second thought, you might have liked
 to be taken by the wind.
I wanted to you in the juice of the fruit,
in delicacy of membrillo and cheese.
I touched you for the last time,
mixed your bones with the aroma of earth
and I think I knelt.
I know you would have
told me to get on with it.
I said a prayer, Mom.
Sweet Lord, I said.

The View

On the north Cascade Highway in the last days
of summer's travel, the car held the road

despite the frost. Trees dusted silver,
landscape purified by darkness.

A woman at the library told us
William Stafford's poems were on a plaque

at Washington Pass. We pulled in.
A small crowd there, though there was hardly traffic.

The pass looked out over a limitless expanse.
We climbed down to the poems poised over the abyss.

"...But maybe sometime you will look out and even
the mountains are gone, the world become nothing..."

Why is it we stop on the curve in the mountains,
the road over the fells with sheep and fields

rising and falling to sunset?
To get a glimpse on the high pass

of a greater landscape, one beyond
the mind, stretching out of the mundane

toward the silence of eternity.

Rubye and the Mule in Bryce Canyon

If you could have chosen your mount
it would have been the buckskin,
the chestnut with a white flash, or little
bay mare with her soft nose and lake eyes.
But you were given the mule,
contrary to what is elegant.
The titanic beast hoofed heavily along the
edge of the path close to the precipice.
The rest climbed sensibly leaning into to rock face.
This long-eared, sure-footed obstinacy
barely skirting the deep abyss...
middle-aged women topped to her death
from a Mule into Bryce Canyon.
The cowboy insisted you continue.
The rest of the party was moving satisfactorily.
It is always the long-eared oppositional mule,
the heavy cargo of ourselves,
that forces us close to the edge.

About the Author

Judith Adams is an English-born poet living on Whidbey Island in Washington State. She has published four books of poetry and recorded several CDs of her work and performances. Her poems have been published in magazines and anthologies and choreographed for dance. Adams has read at the Frye Museum in Seattle, Bainbridge Island Art Museum, Tacoma Art Museum and Northwest Art Museum in Spokane. She has taken poetry to Washington State Correctional Institutions, libraries, state hospitals, theatres, retreat centers, and schools. Adams conducts poetry workshops for youth and adults and most recently leads a Poetry Apothecary for Healing circles. Adams was selected for the Washington State Speakers Bureau.

CPSIA information can be obtained
at www.ICGtesting.com
Printed in the USA
FSHW010720010621
81955FS